*Dire*ct *Experience*
of Reality

Direct Experience of Reality

VERSES FROM THE
APAROKSHANUBHUTI OF
SHRI SHANKARACHARYA
TRANSLATED WITH A
COMMENTARY

by

Hari Prasad Shastri

SHANTI SADAN LONDON

First Edition 1959
Second Impression 1975
Third Impression 1985

ISBN 0-85424-003-9

Published by Shanti Sadan, 29 Chepstow Villas, London W11 3DR

Printed in Great Britain by
Whitstable Litho Ltd.. Whitstable, Kent

Dedicated with love and blessings to

PETER HALLIDAY

whose affectionate friendship has inspired
me to produce this translation of the great
classic of Shri Shankara.

PREFACE

THE philosophy of Advaita Vedanta attributed to Shri Shankara may be compared to the holy Ganges. Even little children can play on its banks, splash its waves upon one another and swim in its little pools of cool and refreshing water; but its depths are so great that even the most practised swimmers seek in vain to touch the bottom.

It may be asked why a philosophy, which in some ways is so simple, can yet be so difficult that it can bewilder even the intellect of a Vachaspati Misra. The reply is that while not every student who wishes to understand Vedanta needs the subtleties of philosophy, yet there are those who delight in them. Besides, we have to keep our mind occupied with something which frees it from the dross of instincts and materialism and elevates it into the atmosphere of inner light and proximity to the infinite spirit.

It is a fact that the advanced thinking of a few distinguished scholars in the realm of philosophy affects the thoughts of people at large. For instance the Darwinian hypothesis of organic evolution was not fully understood by more than a few people in Darwin's own time, but it has since penetrated all the strata of society so thoroughly that today the concepts of evolution, the struggle for existence and the survival of the fittest are familiar everywhere.

PREFACE

The object of a deep study of the holy philosophy is to give the right nourishing food to keen intellects. Some write philosophy, but others find it natural to express their deepest reflections in poetry. Thus the thoughts which Fichte and Herder expressed in their philosophies Goethe conveyed in the form of poetry. In this way the philosophy of contemporary scholars exerts a profound influence on poetry and other branches of culture. This is the *raison d'être* of the philosophy of Vedanta, and it is a purpose which the great Vedantic thinkers such as Shri Harsha Misra and Appaya Dikshit have served very well.

Man is a cultural being. Spengler compares races to organisms and holds that culture is their biography. Music, painting, sculpture and literature are the means of educating people in the refinements of thought, of eliminating the coarser side of their nature and of serving others with forms of lasting beauty. There are many who do not want to go into the analysis of a fruit or to study the details of its species, genus and conditions of growth : they simply want to eat it and enjoy its flavour. But their enjoyment is incomplete unless they add something to express the beauty of the fruit and perhaps to aid its future cultivation.

Advaita Vedanta is more practical than any Western system of philosophy. Its aim is to end for ever the threefold sufferings and to create the light of the spirit within so that the highest and profoundest thoughts may find expression in beauty and rhythm.

For those who wish to have an outline of the

6

holy philosophy and to plunge into its practice in order to direct their personality towards the inner transcendental light, the holy Acharya Shankara has written a few short works. His *Viveka Chudamini* is one of them, but there are some who will find even that great and highly poetical work difficult. Therefore out of his compassion the holy Acharya has written his *Aparokshanubhuti*, ' The Direct Experience of Reality,' which contains an excellent summary of Advaita theory. All that he has expounded in the abstruse commentaries of his philosophical works, Shankara has expressed in this little book in the most simple and beautiful language.

One great service which the holy Acharya has rendered is his dismissal of all the pseudo-Yogas which attract so many people, especially in this part of the world. He has given a symbolic, adhyatmic explanation of the eightfold method of the Sage Patanjali and exposed the futility of asanas, pranayama and other purely physical methods.

One of the opening verses of the *Shrimad Bhagavad* runs : " The fruit pecked by a bird is sweetest. This treatise is the mellowed fruit of the Vedas and Shastras, which are the tree of the philosophy of life." No apter quotation could be found to introduce *Aparokshanubhuti*. It can be said without fear of contradiction that for the earnest student who wishes to understand the holy philosophy and practise it with a view to verify it in his own experience and enjoy the eternal sweetness and freedom of jivanmukti, *Aparokshanubhuti* is perhaps the best guide.

Shri Vidyaranya Swami is said to have written

a commentary on it, but the writer has not seen it, nor has he found it mentioned in any published catalogue of books.

There are a few English translations of this classic already in existence, but they fail to convey its deeper meaning. This new translation of the more important verses with a short commentary has therefore been attempted for the good of members of Shanti Sadan. The savour and true value of this inimitable work will only be appreciated by the reader who does his best to understand and practise its teaching.

HARI PRASAD SHASTRI
30th June, 1955

DIRECT EXPERIENCE OF REALITY

I offer my salutations to Shri Hari, who is all-pervasive, the teacher, the Lord of the universe and the sole cause of all the worlds, whose nature is the highest bliss. [1]

IT is an ancient practice to begin a new work with adoration to the Lord. Sometimes it takes the form of a concise statement of the holy truth as in the first sutra of Shri Vyasa. The object of such an introductory adoration is to eliminate hindrances likely to occur in an exposition of the spiritual truth.

Psychologically speaking, it is a most useful practice to uplift the mind from the illusory region of names and forms to the spiritual transcendence. The verse given above is the subject of meditation of the earnest students of Vedanta. When the mind is stilled and deprived of its associations with names and forms, it becomes fit for the study of truth.

In this verse the Lord, who is both the efficient and the instrumental cause of the universe, is called the teacher and is said to be of the nature of the highest bliss. He is the sole Lord of the universe; He is infinite and all-pervasive. This is a very high conception of the spiritual reality, and it should be kept in mind in the course of our daily life and particularly during the hours of study. Vedanta is not atheistic like southern Buddhism; the Lord is the sole support of the universe, and He is all-pervasive. He is the Christ of the Christians, Allah of the Moslems and Amitabha of the northern Buddhists. The universality of the conception of God in Vedanta is worthy of very serious attention.

The purpose of this book is the achievement of liberation. Good people must take pains to reflect on its contents again and again. [2]

This book is meant to throw light on the path of the liberation of man from the tyranny of limitations, and to give him perfect control over his mind, so enabling him to transcend the limitations of nescience ; this is the only real freedom and, once achieved, it lasts for ever.

People set much store by political freedom, but every institution, whether monarchy, democracy or oligarchy, leads to the tyranny of the few over the many. Man hides his love of power under thousands of veils. There can be no peace in the world or in individual life unless man acquires sovereignty over himself and deals with his fellow-men as extensions of his own Self. In order to establish international peace on a sound basis, the individual must rise above lust, love of wealth, power and pleasure. The only guarantee of such a peace is the realization of the nature of the spirit as the only source of unbroken bliss, freedom and power.

This book is meant for the good. When man has acquired adequate self-control and learnt to subordinate his individual interests to the higher interests of others, has shaken off the tyranny of lust and realised the inability of material objects to give him the satisfaction which his soul seeks, then he is fit to pursue Yoga.

This book is to be reflected upon again and again. As Bergson says, knowledge affects our practical life. It is therefore necessary that the aspirant to perfect bliss and freedom should be a deep student of the philosophy of Advaita. A mere casual reading of a few verses a day and then allowing the mind to wander unrestricted in the dark, deep woods of lust, passion and prejudice, is not the way to the consummation of Yoga.

> *The four essential qualities, detachment and so forth, are acquired by a man who has pleased Shri Hari by performing the duties imposed on him by his station in life and by his profession, and who has practised austerity.* [3].

There are four essential disciplinary qualities, and they are detachment, discrimination, the six virtues beginning with control (shama) and the desire for release. They are not a natural growth in man. Man can be classified according to the four Hindu divisions of labour : scholar, warrior, merchant and worker. Every man must fulfil the duties imposed on him by the scriptures. A duty is that conduct which is obligatory and which is not done for any reward. This division of labour is based on psychological laws and is of great value in a Hindu society and should be so in any society, with slight modifications. Yet the mere performance of duty is not enough. Austerity, such as love of truth, simplicity of living, full control over natural desires, study of the holy scriptures, tolerance, and endurance of the pairs of opposites in equanimity, are also necessary, and they can be acquired by a man who does his best to achieve them in life. Should this be done with any particular aim in view ? Yes, to please Hari, the sole Creator and Governor of the universe, and not for any selfish gain. This is an important point in the Yogic discipline. As nature obeys its Creator and follows the laws imposed by Him, so man must live according to the moral laws and the spiritual regime ordained by God. Man is not a haphazard creation of Nature. By His divine will, called Maya, the Lord has projected the universe out of Himself, like a dream consciously brought forth, and He abides in every particle of it. The end of man's evolution is Godhead. He pleases his Master if he follows the laws imposed by Him.

Freedom of will means adherence to the laws of dharma and the direction of life towards the supreme goal. By living according to the divine will, man receives God's grace and is given the ability to live the fourfold discipline successfully. Whatever a man does, thinks or desires, should be to please the Lord and to follow the laws spiritual, moral and social. One of the chief laws of Yoga is : " All human beings constitute one great family." Devotion includes all the activities of life. Loving remembrance of the Lord all the time is essential.

Vairagya (detachment) is to consider all objects, from Brahma down to the rocks, as worthless from the spiritual point of view. [4]

The word vairagya is often misunderstood. Vedanta is not a philosophy of escapism, nor does it look down on life as a seat of sin. The world is a school where the soul is to be trained to mount higher and higher, the goal being the realization of God as the universal consciousness within. What is condemned in the world is the assumption that there is nothing above or beyond it. Such an attitude towards life produces materialists of the worst type.

Take a schoolboy who loves the garden, benches and walls of his school, but neglects his study. He will be called misled. Similarly a man who thinks that the objects and positions of the world can give him unbroken bliss and freedom is in very great error. In the realm of relativity there is no real bliss and no real freedom. It is a mistake to think that wealth, sex-relationship, power and name have any real value. The duty of a man is to know the nature of his Self and to help his fellow-men. This end is achieved not by hatred of the world but by withdrawal from it together with absorption in benevolence, universal love and knowledge of the nature of the Self. We are all pilgrims to the temple of eternal light which is within the soul. It is a waste of energy to devote oneself to any object of the world exclusively. As long as man is devoted to material objects and his narrow interests, he cannot avoid war, revolution and mass destruction.

Vairagya (detachment) is much needed today.

It is of value not as an end in itself but as a preparatory step to the achievement of truth absolute. If this great principle is adopted in daily life, competition will give place to co-operation, and duplicity and dishonesty will disappear. Vairagya is the foundation of spiritual life.

+.v.a.

The Self is by nature eternal, whereas what is perceived and conceived is not eternal. This idea held with conviction is called the discrimination of the real (viveka). [5]

The second great virtue to be cultivated daily, in order to prepare the mind to receive and keep the light of truth which leads it to freedom and illumination, is spiritual discrimination. There is substance or reality, which is imperishable, untouched by change, unconditioned by space and the law of causation ; it is truth, it is light, and it animates the mind and the senses. To be convinced of the reality of the substance called Atman (Self) and also of the illusory character of the not-Self, the world of conception and perception along with the mind and the senses, is called spiritual discrimination or viveka. The practical application of this great virtue is to avoid being allured by the not-Self, the world, and not to accord to it the status of reality which belongs to the Self. A man who loves a dream can never be happy or free ; but the substratum of the dream is the Self, and it is truth and bliss. The wise detach their mind from the world and apply it to the all-pervasive reality called God or Atman. This is an essential antecedent to self-illumination or release. It implies freedom from desire and aversion. Blessed are those who cultivate the virtue of viveka (discrimination); they will enjoy peace and understand the meaning of the word ' love '.

> *The constant abandonment of desires and ambitions (vasanas) is called inner control (shama). Control of the external senses is called outer control (dama).* [6]

A most important item in the discipline, which prepares the individual soul to win freedom from all miseries and limitations, is mentioned in this verse. The light of the spirit in the form of freedom and bliss is dimmed by desires for profit and gain. He who wants to live in the world as a universal being, jivanmukta, must give up all desires. The light of the infinite God is choked in the human soul by feelings of want, and want is expressed in the form of desire. Can we live without desires ? Yes. When the self is established in the Self, when perfection is sought in the Self and not outside it, the soul reveals its innate bliss. The spirit is perfect; when we attribute desires to it we take it as imperfect. As long as the soul is subject to imperfections, it is conscious of desires. Desires are not always indicative of want. The candidate to higher illumination of the Self must analyse his desires and, first giving up those which are unnecessary, he should then through holy study bring about the total annihilation of all desires.

Outer control of the senses is also essential.

Much of the harm to which society is subjected by its members is due to selfish desires. Imagine the state of society in which the leaders had no power desires but considered all humanity as one family ; it would be heaven on earth. This is what Christ called the Kingdom of Heaven.

The main activity of our present civilisation consists in the creation of new desires and the finding of fresh means to satisfy them. Have our radios and television sets, the casinos of France or the wines of Portugal added to our happiness at all ?

Schopenhauer has explored this subject very well and has recommended the reduction of desires to a minimum as the way to happiness. The race for armaments is mainly due to our search for raw materials and to the necessity of inflicting our commodities on other countries. There is no end to this process, and as long as it continues there will be wars. Dadaji recommended plain living and high thinking. Aristotle sets the highest value on a life of solitary contemplation. The world needs this lesson more than any other.

Turning away from the objects of the senses is called withdrawal (uparati). Bearing the sufferings of life is called endurance (titiksha). [7]

These are the two sovereign virtues of a candidate for spiritual illumination. The mental energy of man is limited, and it is convertible into shanti (peace and illumination). If we spend this energy in the consideration of outer objects, we will have little of it left for higher purposes. By the objects of the senses is meant the unnecessary luxuries of life. A candidate for liberation has to give thought to what he eats, whom he meets, and what he studies ; withdrawal from the necessities of life is impossible. We must create forms of truth and beauty by our thought and by our conduct in society, but not for our own self-pleasure or self-indulgence. If this discipline is observed, we can lead our minds to aesthetic upliftment and right enjoyment and to study, devotion and meditation. To look for any lasting joy in sense-objects is a useless aspiration.

A real man does not run away from the sufferings of the world. They are sure to visit us in the discharge of our moral duties and in the pursuit of the spiritual truth. There is no way of escape. Some people imagine that by retiring from the world they could pursue their life of Yoga better. But unless the mental condition is peaceful and based on right discrimination, they will suffer as much from distraction in solitude as they did in society. The sufferings endured in the discharge of duty, in the performance of study, devotion and meditation, add to the strength of our moral fibre. Not to fear sufferings but to meet them with patience and tranquillity is the chief injunction of the holy Acharya. This is a wonderful teaching, and man needs it more today than ever before. We learn more of the spiritual truth by practising this virtue of endurance than by any other means. Our life in this world will never be free from sufferings ; our mind is ours, and we can discipline it in serenity.

Devoted trust (bhakti) in the words of the holy scriptures and the teacher is called faith (shraddha) ; one-pointedness of the mind on the one real goal of life is called concentration (samadhana). [8]

The scriptures are above logic, though their truth can be established by right reasoning. Unless a pupil has faith in the passages of the scriptures which contain the direct spiritual experiences of the sages, he will remain imprisoned in the web of doubt. Reason cannot solve the doubts a man may have about the authority of experience. Man cannot live without faith in some kind of authority. In Western philosophy reason is assigned the supreme position. Our holy Acharyas believe in reason (tarka), but they are not slaves to it. The philosophy which is based on reason alone is as changeable as a weather-cock in the wind. Aristotle held his domain for over a thousand years ; but he was overthrown by the appearance of new systems of reasoning and experiment. When Hegel offered his philosophy in the last century, many accepted it as the last word. Nowadays Bertrand Russell calls Hegelianism a tissue of errors from A to Z.

Reason functions in the realm of duality. Its functions are analytic and synthetic, but it is powerless in the realm of non-duality. Students of history, geography and physics take for granted the statements of the authors of their text-books. William James, Bergson and many other brilliant intellects of our time do not think the intellect competent to judge the highest truth.

Thus in matters spiritual the Shruti claims full authority. The ancient texts are explained by a competent teacher. To defend the statements of the Shruti, Shri Shankara Acharya, who is held to be the greatest dialectician in the world, uses reasoning of a most subtle kind. We do not discount the use of reasoning but accord it its rightful place. In fact, great emphasis is laid by Shri Shankara on the value of vichara (ratiocination) in the philosophy of Advaita, an exact system of thought in which logic plays a most important part. Many classics have been written to establish the truth of the Shruti by reasoning, such as *Advaita Siddhi* of Shri Madhusudana Sarasvati and the great works of Shri Harsha Misra and Vachaspati Misra.

Another important item of discipline is to focus the mind wholly on the goal of life, the spiritual awakening of man.

> " *O all-pervasive Lord, when and how shall I be freed from the bondage of this ever-changing world?* " *This aspiration firmly fixed in the intellect is called the desire for release* (*mumuk-shuta*). [9]

Some are pessimists, some are optimists, while some call themselves realists and try to transform the world into a source of perennial joy and freedom. Indeed it is commonly held that this is possible. In mid-Victorian times scientific advance and constitutional reform on democratic lines were held to be sure means to real progress in peace, prosperity and freedom. But so far the world has not become any less dangerous for man. Science is being exploited to destroy mankind for political ends; the ideal of democracy is merely a tool in the hands of self-seeking politicians. Is man doomed to suffering and bondage for ever? Must we accept the conclusions of the materialists and believe in the non-existence of Providence?

There is another school of thought which holds that above the clouds of ignorance the sun of happiness and liberty shines in full splendour. The world does not affect the whole of human personality; the essence of man's existence is truth. The reforms of the realm of ignorance have a certain meaning, but they do not touch truth absolute. The limitations under which man works imply the existence of a state of consciousness beyond all limitations. The spirit being infinite and absolute is imprisoned phenomenally in the realm of nescience. The sages have gone beyond it and do so even today. Has this philosophy any social application? Is it escapism, as Albert Schweitzer holds? No, not at all. The good Schweitzer's approach is unphilosophical as he has hermetically sealed his intellect against any expression of truth other than narrow Christianity. The application of the philosophy of Advaita to our daily life begins with the idea of the brotherhood of man and the fatherhood of God. The world is a school in which we learn how to practise virtue and live with all in peace and brotherly love. There is no instance in the history of the world of a statesman, conqueror or humanist who can say what the adherents of

Advaita have emphatically declared: "I have found all that was to be found; I have known all that was to be known; I am at one with the highest good". This state of truth is open to anyone who cares to study and discipline himself with a view to its attainment. The holy Acharya here gives expression to this state of the mind. It consists in the desire to end the darkness of limitations and to enjoy for ever the light of the spirit. This aspiration must occupy the first place in our heart.

The man who is endowed with the disciplinary qualities mentioned above and is devoted to the highest good ought to exercise his faculty of reflection and ratiocination to achieve the knowledge of truth. [10]

The highest good is the vision of truth eternal and imperishable in a man's own Self. A candidate for this exalted state of Self-illumination must equip himself with the qualifications mentioned in the above verses, and then exercise his faculty of thought to separate the chaff of unreality and illusion from the grain of truth. The vision is not obtained through any other means but calm and deep reflection. Here lies the importance of the exercise of logic and reasoning.

Many candidates to the divine vision within want to obtain peace and illumination but neglect the great discipline laid down in these verses. They will not obtain the divine consciousness. Some people begin to find fault with Yoga's promise of liberation. Many immature souls take to the study of Vedanta under the impression that they can acquire spiritual perfection and at the same time enjoy the pleasures of the sense objects. They will miserably fail. Renunciation is the keynote of the divine music. Mere logic-chopping or the blind reflections of men who believe in nonsensical systems lead nowhere in the divine realm.

As in the absence of physical light the objects are not revealed, so the realization of the Self (jnana) is not obtained without cogitation (vichara). [11]

An objection sometimes raised by those who have only a nodding acquaintance with Vedanta is that it is based on dogmatism and cannot therefore be called a rational system. In this verse supreme importance is assigned to reflection by rational means on the Vedantic truth postulated by the holy Shruti. A man may be charitable and do good to others and even practise external devotion in the form of rituals, but for direct realization he must perform ratiocination. Self-analysis is a very important element in the cognition of the reality within. The method of self-analysis is like the method used by Euclid in geometry. Faith plays an important part even in logic. Unless a student has faith in the competence of logic to reveal truth, he cannot undertake a rational enquiry into it; he does not try to prove the competence of proof. Logical rules are taken for granted. Mind cannot reveal the truth but it can help to establish it by logic and proper reasoning. Logic can also be abused, as it is by the supporters of dialectical materialism. This is an important point and merits careful examination. Those who want to make a further study of this aspect of Vedanta are referred to the works of Shri Harsha Misra, Shri Vachaspati Misra and the great Madhusudana Sarasvati.

" What am I? How is the world created?
Who is its creator? What is its material cause? "
This is the reasoning called cogitation (vichara).
[12]

Sometimes unproductive logic-chopping is described as vichara. In the contests of logic known as Nyaya Shastra, in which I used to participate in my student days in Benares, hours would be spent in controversy on subjects far removed from any practical bearing, and yet this was called vichara. This verse gives a typical example of true vichara (cogitation). The chief function of a knower is to know himself. Am I matter or mind, or something other than these two? What is this world spread out before me in time and space? How has it been caused? Is it a machine created by itself? Or is it the work of a Creator? If so, what is His nature? What is the stuff of which the world is created? These are most important questions because on the answer to them depends the choice of the ideal to be pursued in life. This is an enquiry into the enquirer. It should be conducted independently and on logical lines. It is an excellent practice in the application of thought.

We can deduce our right conduct in society from our answers to these questions. Now follow a few conclusions from this sort of cogitation which a student has to verify for himself by his own reasoning.

> "*I am not the body, which is a combination of material elements, nor am I a collection of the senses. I am something different from both these.*"
> *This is the reasoning called cogitation (vichara).*
> [13].

Here is a further illustration of vichara, which does not mean unbridled reasoning. If one gives full rein to the mind, the result is sure to be chaos. Cogitation has to be performed within certain well-defined limits. It is an attempt to focus the mind on the outer fringe of the Self, where it can receive more of the spiritual light and be rendered fit for absorption in the spirit. This kind of cogitation can be said to be dynamic meditation and is a method whereby the mind does the negative work necessary to prepare itself for deeper meditation on the Self. Shri Bhagavadpad Acharya shows how to make the best use of the logical faculty. When a man is convinced that he is fundamentally spirit and not body and mind, great ethical ends are served; detachment becomes easy and natural, and the mind can no longer be imprisoned in the love of names and forms and appearances.

"I am not a collection of senses". How can this be known? Because I am the subject, the witness of the mind and the senses. The subject is entirely different from the object. It is clear that the perceiver is not the perceived. In the final analysis of the personality it is found that even the empirical perceiver is in the realm of avidya (nescience), the not-Self. When Aristotle in the concluding part of his Metaphysics speaks of a life devoted to the contemplation of the Reality in perfect detachment as the ideal life, he means the sort of cogitation which is described here by the holy Acharya. A new world is revealed to the Yogi by the practice of this method. His mind is absorbed in a serenity in which all other joys are infinitely surpassed.

" The whole world is a product of nescience ; it disappears on the dawn of true knowledge. Its real creator is the mental activity (sankalpa) of many kinds." This is the reasoning called cogitation (vichara). [14]

In this verse the holy Acharya lays down a prominent principle of the philosophy of Vedanta. Two questions were asked in the previous verse : " What is this world ? " and " Who is its creator ? " The world is a creation of nescience in the form of the various activities of the mind. What is this nescience ? It is a principle which is positive and beginningless, but which can cease to exist. As the mind itself, which thinks and wills and feels, is a modification of this nescience, it cannot know it. Here the creation is said to be a product of the mind. This is the cornerstone of the philosophy. Nescience is neither real nor unreal. If it were real it would continue for ever and there could then be no possibility of release from its bonds or limitations. In that case all practice of righteousness, devotion and learning would be useless. If this position is accepted as true, then how can we account for the desire of the soul of man to be free from all limitations? Everyone wants to be happy and longs for a state of happiness which has no end. When this desire is enveloped by ignorance, we imagine that youth, health, wealth reputation and sex-love can give happiness. Is there no end to this process of becoming? Yes, there is. When the spirit is freed from its relationship with the mind in the state called enlightenment (jnana), the world as a conglomeration of conditions disappears like the mirage river in the desert. The world exists in the mind and is a product of the mind. Here the word 'mind' covers both its aspects, macrocosmic and microcosmic; the human mind imposes its sub-creation on the projection of the cosmic mind.

Real vichara means cogitation on this line of thought. Endless dialectics are permitted in the course of this vichara. We study both Eastern and Western philosophy, by way of comparison.

"*As clay is the material cause of a pot, so is the subtle, imperishable truth absolute the material cause of nescience (ajnana) and thought (sankalpa).*" *This is the reasoning called cogitation (vichara).* [15]

Nescience (ajnana), of which the mental and physical worlds are a modification, has no independent existence. It is not a modification of truth (Brahman). It is a phenomenal superimposition (vivarta) on Brahman. Thought, which is not gross or material but a subtle form of the original nescience, is also a modification of ajnana.

Western philosophy hardly ever looks beyond the sphere of thought. Plato and Hegel postulate a spirit and an Absolute which are not different from a higher phase of mind. Truth lies in the transcendent region beyond the mind. All modifications of nescience are perishable, ever-changing and illusory; but Truth (Brahman) is imperishable, ever unconditioned and most subtle. It is called subtle because it is beyond the grasp of the mind and speech. This is a very abstruse doctrine of Advaita Vedanta, and it is only through very deep cogitation that one can understand it.

"*It is a most undoubted fact that I am the One who is subtle, the cogniser, the witness, truth and imperishable*". This is the reasoning called cogitation (*vichara*). [16]

The starting point of our daily reflection is the conception of the unity of all that is. Our earth is a detail of our solar system, which is in itself one of billions which fill this universe. Each atom is animated by the universal mind, which in its turn draws its light and inspiration from the spirit which is non-dual and all bliss. Man, from the subjective point of view, is a detail of this infinite, most majestic spirit. In practical life this conviction, which is based on reason and scientific investigation, leads one to the belief in a universal brotherhood far above rational and artificial sub-divisions. There is no room for hedonism or individual enjoyment of life divorced from the good of the whole. All may not appear to be good at present. The shadows are many, but the substance is one. When man, the spirit, moves his mind with universal love and co-operation, he serves the whole. Any other kind of thinking, whether of a Karl Marx or an Adam Smith, is partial and not whole.

We must meditate on this verse. The spirit is subtle, that is, not within the range of the senses or the intellect. It is indestructible because it transcends time-space. The Yogi is enjoined to reflect on this idea in inner calmness. No arguments to establish the fact are to be entertained, because the sphere of reasoning is far below the spiritual sphere. The maturity of this conviction is proved by spiritual living in our practical life. This is the highest prayer and a prelude to spiritual worship. A study of *Vira Vijaya* should accompany this kind of cogitation.

> *Self (Atman) is one and without parts, while the body is composed of many parts. To see the identity of the two—what ignorance can be greater than this?* [17]

A new topic is opened in this verse, that of discrimination between the Self and the body. All our misery is due to our identification of the Self with the body. The bodies are many : the Self is one. As one and the same moon appears as many when reflected in jars filled with water, so the same Self appears as many when conditioned in the bodies. The Self is simple : the bodies are compound. The Self is fixed and self-effulgent : the bodies are many and each is constantly changing. The bodies are by nature inert: the Self is vital in its own splendour. It is clear that the Self is not the body. This error can be removed by reflecting on the truth that the Self is different from the body. When this truth is realised, the body will continue to change, but the Self will remain unaffected, one and pure.

> *The Self is the ruler and inner dweller : the body is external and subject to control. To see the identity of the two—what ignorance can be greater than this ?* [18]

The same theme—amazement over the identity of the body and the spirit which is entertained by the ignorant—is continued in this verse. It speaks of the characteristic differences of the two. The Self is not just the witness, as is held by the Sankhya philosophers ; in one of its aspects it is the ruler of the body. This is a reference to the verse in the *Kena Upanishad*: " By whose will does the mind work and the vitality move ? " The mind is an instrument of the Self. If it is disciplined, stilled and purified, it is a useful servant ; but if it is left in identification with the body, it becomes a source of suffering and darkness. The Self is manifest within the body as the flame in the chimney of an oil lamp. To see the identity of the two is the height of ignorance. The holy Acharya does not maintain the distinction between the body and the spirit on scriptural grounds only; he makes full use of logic and reasoning to convince the spirit clouded with ignorance that the two are dissimilar.

> *The Self is knowledge by nature and pure : the body is composed of flesh and is impure. To see the identity of the two—what ignorance can be greater than this ?* [19]

This verse again emphasizes the complete separateness of the Self from the body. In its secondary meaning the word ' ajnana ' (absence of true knowledge) means confusion between the body and the Self. By meditating on the text given above and by paying due attention to truth and virtue, one comes to realize that the Self is pure and knowledge itself by nature. The saint and the sinner can both perform their tasks under the light of the same lamp, which shines impartially on all. Extroversion and introversion, sin and sorrow, virtue and merit do not belong to the witnessing Self.

This meditation gives to the soul an undisturbed peace and spiritual edification which are unsurpassed. In our daily devotions we should revolve these verses in our mind and reproduce them in great spiritual peace in our daily life.

> *The Self is eternal and truth itself (sat) : the body is temporal and unreal (asat). To see the identity of the two—what ignorance can be greater than this ?* [21]

The spiritual truth contained in this verse is meant

for our daily meditation. The great Rishi of modern times, Swami Rama Tirtha, has said that Vedanta is meant for each and everyone and not only for a select few. Shri Shankara also has said that anyone who wants to eliminate his suffering is entitled to the truth of Vedanta. It is useless to take Vedanta as a luxury, something only to be talked about for intellectual satisfaction; it is meant to convert our mind into the spiritual consciousness.

It is due to the light of the Self that objects appear to exist. The effulgence of the Self is not like that of physical fire, as is shown by the darkness at night. [22]

One of the great doctrines of Advaita is embodied in this verse. It is hard to understand before Self-realization, although the great philosophers of Advaita have given the strongest arguments in support of it. Objects, including the sun, appear on account of the light of the Self. They have no independent luminosity. How does the cognition of the sun take place? It is clear that the Self and the human mind are not illumined by the physical sun. It is the Self which cognizes the sun's rise at dawn and its meridian at noon. The Self also perceives the absence of the sun at night. The Self is self-revealed at all times whether physical light is present or not. This may only be an intellectual inference at first, but it becomes evident when the Self-illumination of Atman is realised in the inner peace.

It is strange that the deluded, although always knowing the body to be theirs and not themselves as in the perception of a pot, still identify themselves with it. [23]

In this verse emphasis is laid on the realization of the cardinal truth which proclaims the independence of the spirit from the body and the mind. The subject has been discussed in the previous few verses. The spiritual peace and eternal bliss, which follow the realization of this truth in practical life, are discovered to be the nature of the Self through discipline, devotion and meditation. In order to emphasize this point, the holy Acharya has stressed its importance over and over again. To have decentralized the spirit from the false egoity is an achievement of the highest order. It is the task which faces the earnest and serious student of Yoga. The philosophy of Yoga is based on realism and is highly practical. Its truth is verifiable in daily life.

" *I am Brahman, ever the same and most peaceful, by nature reality, consciousness and bliss. I am not the body, which is ever changing and unreal.*" *This the wise call knowledge (jnana).* [24]

The essence of human life is knowledge or higher cognition, which the soul embraces in order to live wisely and well and to promote the good of others. The conviction which is the essence of religion and philosophy, which is the highest truth and which manifests itself in our daily life in great peace and restfulness and inner equilibrium, is contained in the verse given above. This is not a goal to be attained but it is already a fact, an undisputed and undeniable fact. The body is called unreal, not in the sense of a dream or the son of a barren woman, but in the sense that it has no independent existence. The body is an instrument to aid the embodied intelligence to work out its own salvation and to help others to do the same. Men with a narrow Christian bias are scared of the idea of the unreality of the body. They are far more body-conscious than spirit-conscious. If the body were real, then the spirit, which is diametrically opposed to the body, could not be real too. If the dream were real, the waking consciousness would be unreal. The body exists by virtue of existence and not vice versa. Much philosophical confusion has been caused by the alleged resurrection of the body of Christ. I am sure Christ never meant this to be taken literally. It is the spirit which is eternal and which is absolutely opposed to the body in its great qualities. In pursuit of the higher ethics we have to sacrifice many of the demands of the body. Belief in the immortality of the body is a negation of God and rank materialism. When they say Christ rose from the dead, they forget that the spirit never dies and that Christ was the spirit.

" Unmodifiable, formless, without blemish, imperishable am I. I am not the body, which is ever changing and unreal." This the wise call knowledge. [25]

This is another text for meditation with feeling. It

is not an intellectual text and the peace which follows reflection upon it is the outcome of the positive assertion of the absolute reality of the Self. This assertion is not permanent in the antahkarana of a Yogi, but the intellect is coloured by the deeper aspect of its meaning. If the antahkarana is reduced to the state of Advaita all the time, which it cannot be on account of the presence of rajas in it, the jnani will not be able to eat, sleep or teach. In the case of experiences which are common both to the jnani and the ajnani, the jnani is equanimous and rooted in the conviction of the unreality of appearances. To assert that the mind can be held in the state of Advaita in every condition of daily life is merely a pretence. How could the Lord drive the chariot of his nephew Prince Arjuna in battle and keep His mind on the perfect absolute Advaita at the same time? In the practical state called vyavaharika, the jnani follows the injunction of the Gita : " Eating, sleeping, talking . . . he knows he is not doing anything ".

Many who have not fully grasped the meaning of Advaita confuse the state of practical experience (sansara) with the state of absolute Brahman. Nowhere is it stated that the world does not exist. It does exist, but its existence is phenomenal, and the jnani is not deluded by the play of events.

" *Untouched by suffering, beyond all illusory appearances and free from doubt and indecision (nirvikalpa), I am all-pervasive ; I am not the body which is ever changing and unreal." This the wise call knowledge.*" [26]

" I am without attributes, actionless, eternal,
ever free and indestructible ; I am not the body
which is ever changing and unreal." This the
wise call knowledge. [27]

" I am taintless, immovable, infinite, pure, free
from old age and death ; I am not the body which
is ever changing and unreal." This the wise
call knowledge." [28]

O simpleton, why dost thou regard as nothing
(shunya) thy Self, which is called Purusha, is
lovable and, as declared by the scriptures, abides
in the body but is independent of it ? [29]

When philosophers search for a means to pure and
abiding happiness, they are asked to look within and
know the nature of the spirit which is free from all
taints and which, though abiding in the body, is in
no way tainted by its inertia and other limitations.
It is the source of supreme beauty. The physical
beauty of nature, form, art and science, is not
independent of the spirit but is a reflection of it.
When the spirit knows itself as radically different
from the body and the mind, then it knows the
real beauty which does not fade and which is
called truth.

This hypothesis of the Self being supreme beauty,
truth and bliss is found in the holy scriptures, but
it must be verified in one's own direct experience
by the practice of selfless benevolence, devotion
and meditation. Faith in a creed is of value only

when it prepares the soul of the enquirer to verify its truth in his own experience. From this point of view, insistence on an empirical creed has little spiritual value. " Why dost thou regard thy Self as nothing ? " means that it is wrong and a source of infinite danger and distress to think, as do the Buddhist Madhyamikas, that the Self does not exist or that it is a void (shunya).

> *Learn from the Shruti and through reasoning of the nature of thy Self, which is truth, which transcends the body and which is seen by the dull-witted like thee with difficulty.* [30]

Owing to delusion created by the limitations called Maya, a dull-witted man finds it hard to know the nature of the Self. It is clear from this statement of the holy Acharya that the Self is hard to know but not unknowable. It is said to be beyond the body and the mind, and therefore neither the senses nor the mind are capable of perceiving it. The first indication of the truth about Atman is found in the statements of the holy Shruti. But we are also offered reasoning in support of Shruti. The function of reasoning is to elucidate the statements of Shruti and to meet the opponent's objections. In Vedanta, logic is not excluded from the consideration of the student but plays a very important part.

Self cannot be proved because it is the inner light under which the proving process itself takes place, but it is self-evident as ' I am.' The objections of the opponent, whether a materialist like Charvaka or a dualist like the followers of Sankhya or Nyaya, can be successfully met on logical grounds. That which cannot be taken on faith is defended by reasoning and logic.

> *Indicated by the personal pronoun 'I' abides the transcendental Self, one and only one. How can the physical bodies which are many be the Self?* [31]

For the reasons given above the radical difference between the nature of the spirit and the body is apparent. In a few subsequent verses (not translated here) this theme is developed.

> *The Self, which is in fact the Lord and which is called Purusha because it abides in the body, is different from the physical and subtle bodies. I am that spirit. I am the Self of all. I am all, imperishable and beyond all.* [40]

The doctrinal aspect of Advaita is established by logic and reasoning, but not everyone is fond of logic. In the holy philosophy the chief function of logic is to refute the objections of dualists, atheists and materialists. The main purpose of these texts is to help the Jiva in the realization of the Self through deep meditation. Meditation is not successful without discipline and devotion. The devotion here recommended is the identificative one.

The social and moral implications of this doctrine

are clear. The doctrine of the unity of the spirit is the foundation of all morality, both social and individual. No one tries to harm himself; so how can one who knows that each and every living being is his own Self harm anybody? There is no room here for narrow nationalism or psychological individualism. The greatness of the doctrine of Advaita makes nonsense of all war, social exploitation and desire to achieve national superiority; it strikes at the roots of social and individual evils and leaves no room for international friction; it permits no inquisition, but gives freedom to each and everyone to live a life of righteousness.

Consciousness (chaitanya) is ever the same; there is no possibility of difference within it. Like the illusory appearance of a snake in a rope, the condition of the Jiva is illusory in pure consciousness. [43]

There are no degrees and no points of difference whatsoever in consciousness absolute, which is one without a second. Any other thing, whether the outer world of time and space or the inner world of mental harmony and disturbance, has no real existence in consciousness. Whatever is conceived or perceived, whether the heaven of Allah with its countless houris or the Buddhist hell filled with man-eating alligators, is all mere appearance, mere words without meaning, absolutely devoid of any essential reality. As a rope appears as an illusory snake, so pure consciousness appears as the world to the Jiva.

DIRECT EXPERIENCE

As through want of knowledge of the rope it appears for a moment as a snake, so owing to nescience pure consciousness appears in the form of the world. [44]

One of the objects of philosophy is to explain the world and to remove man's subjective confusion and restlessness with a view to promote creative peace and undisturbed bliss. Man is a thinking being, and he is his true Self when he asks such questions as : " What is this world ? What is its meaning and purpose ? What is its cause ? " From Plato to Bertrand Russell so many thinkers have produced theories to explain the world, but the most rational explanation of the world is given by the philosophers of Advaita. The world is not brushed aside as a dream or as something unreal like the son of a barren woman. In his criticisms of Eastern idealism Albert Schweitzer reveals gross ignorance of the Advaita teaching.

If appearances are to be taken as real, then why do they change ? Why do they give satisfaction today but not tomorrow, and why do various people have various views about them ? The reality of a thing does not depend on its appearance. Is the sky blue ? Do the horizons meet ? Is the world flat ? Besides, if appearances are real and correct, then what about existence absolute in which they subsist like the changing clouds in the ether ? This truth is not easily grasped by a matter-of-fact materialistic mind. Has materialism ever produced a man of spiritual calm (shanti) ? Were the great creators like Valmiki, Shakespeare,

Goethe, Beethoven and Michelangelo materialists?

The explanation of the world given in this verse is from the point of view of Advaita Vedanta. The mind has two phases, knowledge and ignorance. Ignorance creates dreams, knowledge reveals truth. In this verse the august and holy Acharya says that reality or consciousness appears as the world to a soul under the sway of nescience. The world is an erroneous representation of the eternal reality of consciousness. This point of view is opposed to the nihilism of the deluded Buddhists.

> *There is no other material cause of the universe than Brahman ; this whole world therefore is in fact Brahman and nothing else.* [45]

This is the cardinal doctrine of the holy philosophy. The only end of human life is to realise its truth in daily life. How are we to overcome fear, defeat, death and turn the terror of the grave into the serenity of summer moonlight? It is by meditating upon the truth in this verse and so acquiring transcendental peace and happiness. This is not merely the plausible theory of a philosopher like Hegel but a matter of intuitive experience. The stilled and purified mind which recognises the truth contained in this verse is absorbed by contemplation in the infinite light of the Self. Then follows natural peace and bliss.

The content of thousands of books of philosophy is contained in this one verse of Shri Shankara's. This is the end of the study of philosophy and of the life of devotion and discipline. However hard and extrovertive and restless the mind may be, it is never dead to the possibility of appreciating the spiritual truth. Material and emotional gains are mere show with no reality behind them. At any cost a man must realise the truth contained in this verse.

" All is Self," says the holy Shastra. It cannot be said that the world is pervaded by Brahman. When this high truth is known no room is left for any feeling of difference. [46]

There are some thinkers who hold that the world is made of matter but that it is pervaded by Brahman just as our human body is pervaded and supported by vitality. This theory is rejected in the philosophy of Advaita. The great truth is that all is Brahman. When this truth is intellectually recognised and intuitively perceived, then all feelings of difference end for ever.

Sin and sorrow are the results of the feeling of duality. The holy Advaita destroys the feeling of duality by postulating the non-duality of Brahman and jagat. No room is left for grief or joy ; and there is no possibility of any immoral feeling or action when the unity of all that is perceived and conceived is intuitively experienced.

This is an important verse, and meditation on it helps the rise of the feeling of non-duality. It is by deep meditation accompanied by a feeling of detachment (vairagya) that the unity of the Self, God and the world is realised. Study is helpful, and so is devotion ; but the final essence of the holy philosophy is the feeling of Advaita.

The Shruti points out the great error of multi-
plicity which leads the Jiva from death to death.
Man, deceived by Maya, sees multiplicity in
sansara. [48]

A very important truth is declared by the most
holy Acharya in this verse. The vision of multiplicity, which is the root cause of suffering and
which leads to the continuation of the individualised
life from birth to death and then to rebirth, is
caused by the various manifestations of erroneous
perception and conception which make up the
universe. This is considered to be the very
foundation of all sin and sorrow in sansara. Some-
body will say: "What about joy in sansara?
What about the conquest of Persia by Alexander of
Macedon? What about the joy of Napoleon's
victory over Russia and Prussia at Austerlitz? Is
not a honeymoon a joyful period?" No. These
joys are so short-lived, so dreamlike and so sure to
be followed by pain, that the wise do not care for
them. What about the thousands and thousands of
young men who perished in these battles? Were
they joyful? Did their families rejoice over their
deaths? Sooner or later a honeymoon reveals
difference of outlook, and disagreement and dissen-
sion arise. A tasty French dinner leads to gastric
disorders. If carefully studied, the joys of life are
seen to be like fire-flies flickering in a dark night.
Duality in conception and perception leads only to
pain and sorrow and not to real joy.

Maya is the veiling power, and under it the soul
sees multiplicity and consequently suffers.

DIRECT EXPERIENCE

*All beings are born of Brahman who is the
supreme spirit; they are therefore Brahman.
Be convinced of this.* [49]

This verse contains the greatest truth to which a
man can aspire. The dialectical evidence in support of it is overwhelming. From the great
Sureshwara to the holy Paramahansa Rama Tirtha,
thousands of pages of the closest arguments have
been written in its confirmation. If you can take it
on faith, so much the better for you; but if you
want to verify it by reasoning and logic, then turn
to the great and mighty dialecticians of Advaita
such as Chitsukhacharya, Vidyaranya Swami and
Madhusudana Saraswati. Science, too, in its
own way supports the doctrine of Advaita to a
great extent. In my youth when I was a student
of physics and biology, the name of Ernest Haeckel
was the greatest in science. He called himself a monist
and repudiated dualism in the realm of science.

There is an Arabic verse " I alone exist and none
else," which is eloquent with the same truth.
Enjoy meditation on this holy truth in your calmer
moments; all worries and anxieties, all fears and
doubts, will be dispelled like bats by the sunlight.
Virtue in its highest form has the support of this
truth. All being the one Self, whom shall we hate,
whom shall we consider a stranger? All being
one, the highest expression of love is to be devoted
to the one infinite Self shining through your mind,
through the being of an amoeba, through the lotuses
smiling in the early sunlight and swaying in the
breeze. When the life of a Yogi is coloured by

this idea of non-duality, his mind blossoms and the light of consciousness shines forth as the light of bliss, both being one and the same.

All names, all forms and all actions are supported by Brahman. So speaks the holy Shruti. [50]

Sometimes it is said that names and forms are unreal and at other times it is said that all is Brahman. Is this not a contradiction ? No. The rings, chains and bangles made of gold are all gold, though the names given to the modifications of gold are unreal. For convenience we can say that all is Brahman, but when the modifications of gold are taken as independent of gold and are called real, the Shruti is quoted to remind us of the real position of Vedanta. There is no contradiction in the Shruti. When we mature our meditation on non-duality, we consign the unreal to non-existence and speak of the substratum as real, as existence. It is in this sense that all is Brahman. Imagine a rope lying on the ground. One man takes it to be a snake, another a crack in the earth, another a line of water on the ground. But the man who knows it is only a rope says : " All that each of you sees is a rope ". This is the meaning of Shruti when it says : " All is Brahman ".

The dull-witted man who persists in making even the least distinction between the embodied spirit (Jiva) and the spirit absolute (Brahman) is subject to fear. The Shruti points this out. [52]

Philosophy must have a pragmatic aspect. If it

keeps our mind in the air and does not show us its practical value in fearlessness, it is not of much use. Take the subjective idealism of Buddhism : it leads the mind into chaos and innumerable difficulties and gives no value to our daily life. To Shri Shankara the relative world is not unreal as it is to the Buddhist school. Fear is our greatest enemy ; it cripples our judgement and robs us of all initiative to do good and to make investigation into truth. In unity there is no fear. As long as a wave thinks that it is different from water or from the other waves, it is afraid of destruction and is subject to malice and ambition. But when it has realised " I am water," it is above fear and the idea of destruction. So is one who knows Brahman.

It is the perception of duality due to ignorance which produces the feeling of separateness. Multiplicity is swept away when all is seen to be of the nature of the Self. The Mahatma who realises this truth and knows the Self to be common to all beings is free from delusion and grief owing to the destruction of duality. [53 and 54].

The spiritual truth, which when known demolishes the feelings of multiplicity and attachment to objects, is beautifully and succinctly expressed in this verse. When a man is perfectly healthy he is unconscious of any duality in any part of his body and is happy ; but as soon as duality is caused by a little headache or indigestion or inflammation, the suffering individual becomes conscious that his body is made up of different parts.

The word ' moha,' translated as ' delusion,' means a wrong impression of an object caused by a misunderstanding or a want of understanding of its nature. The peace of the individual is destroyed when such an innocent object as a rope is taken to be a snake. So also the feeling ' This is mine and mine alone ' creates a feeling of duality and leads to endless grief. The writer has opposed the sentiment of narrow nationalism because it is based on ignorance not only of spiritual facts but also of anthropological and biological facts. This verse records a most valuable dictum : man must decentralise his egoity and realise the illusion of separateness based on colour, race, and creed. This is the only way to become conscious of the truth of unity and enjoy unbroken peace.

How valuable is the message of the holy Shruti which stresses the truth of the unity of all in God ! When so much money and energy are wasted on armaments and commercial luxury, which lead only to greater and greater sufferings, it is time for some individuals to devote themselves to the study, realization and propagation of the philosophy of Shri Shankara. Great dangers threaten the world, not only from the hydrogen bomb but also in connection with racial questions based on colour and differences of language and geography. Has humanity yet atoned for the great cruelty inflicted on the noble Jewish race for no valid reasons at all ?

The highest knowledge, which can bring nations and sects together and weave them into a chaplet of unity, is the philosophy of Advaita.

The Greek and Roman civilizations were based

on slavery. Today Marxist communism divides the world into two hostile camps, the proletariat and the bourgeoisie. Such methods are wrong and unnatural: as the Shruti says, all is Brahman.

Though it is experienced and though it is serviceable in relativity, this world, which contradicts itself in successive moments, is unreal like a dream. [56]

The unreality of the world is a recognised factor in the spiritual experience. An object which changes every moment, sometimes in its parts and sometimes radically, is like a dream and is consequently unreal. It is not unreal like the son of a barren woman, because it has a practical reality. Still, being opposed to the timeless entity called Brahman, which is not subject to the law of causation, the world cannot but be called unreal. If the world were said to be real, it would be a unilateral conception and there would be nothing unreal. A little consideration will show that the spirit, which is immutable because it is above time and immortal because it is not subject to the law of causation, can be the only reality. Some people think that the world's being unreal leaves man with no responsibilities and no moral obligations. This is not so. Whatever causes affliction has to be negated. There are degrees of unreality, and although the world is not absolutely unreal, yet as it causes fear, want of peace and ignorance of the eternal truth of the spirit, it is to be thoroughly understood. Let it also be remembered that a dream headache is cured by a dream medicine. Similarly, the performance of our social, moral and spiritual duties helps the recognition of the un-reality of the world and produces a conviction of the reality of the spirit, which is the illusory world's substratum.

> *As a man when he has known their origin does not see the illusory jar in the clay or the silver in the mother-of-pearl, so the illumined man does not see Jivahood in Brahman.* [59]

The Advaita Vedanta explains that the relation of the world to the ultimate reality is similar to the relation of a clay jar to clay. The jar is in no way different from the clay, and yet a deluded man does not take the clay into account but imposes the name, form and colour of the jar on the clay. These attributes of the jar are not real, and they have no existence apart from the clay ; similarly, the world and all our relationships with it is nothing but the ultimate reality (Brahman). Some philosophers in the West have advanced theories which resemble Advaita, but they do not have the same practical result as Advaita, that is, the negation of fear in whatever form. It is the highest speculative achievement of the philosophy of Shri Bhagavadpad Shankara that the seer, the perceiver of the pheno-menal world, is recognised as Brahman, the ultimate reality, pure and simple. It is not held that the perceiving entity is transformed into the ultimate reality.

Another illustration is that of the silver seen

erroneously in mother-of-pearl. Many objections have been made against the position of Advaita. It is said, for instance, that there is real silver apart from mother-of-pearl, and that the imagination imposes the real silver on the mother-of-pearl. Where is the real world, it may then be asked, which is imposed on Brahman? The objection seems powerful, but this and many others like it have been ably and satisfactorily refuted by the great Acharyas of Advaita.

> *As a jar exists in clay, an ear-ring in gold and silver in mother-of-pearl, but all only nominally, so in word only does the Jiva exist in Brahman.*
> [60]

In philosophy we try to find an explanation of the Self, the world and God. The dualistic systems, like the Cartesian philosophy in the West, assert the independent existence of these three categories. They devote thousands of pages to the analysis of the differences between them and to explanations of the purpose of creation, but in fact they only lead their readers from complication to complication. Though their ethics are not too weak, their metaphysics break down. In this verse Shri Shankara describes so tersely and well the relationship between God and the individual soul.

This is one of the grandest messages of all philosophy : it proclaims the real independence, majesty and perfection of the individual soul, which is declared to be identical with the universal spirit. God is all-pervasive, and this could not be so if the soul and matter had an independent existence,

If God pervaded the soul and matter as electricity pervades a heating element, He would be limited and therefore subject to change. Immortality could not be ascribed to such an entity. Moreover, on this theory the problem of the origin of matter from God, who is consciousness, remains inexplicable. How could dry sand be the product of water? How could inanimate matter, so radically opposed in all its aspects to the spirit, be a creation of the spirit or God? Therefore the theory of vivarta, the phenomenal superimposition of the world on the spirit, is the most rational. Besides, it adds to the real dignity of man to be proclaimed identical with God. By close and incontrovertible reasoning the theory of vivarta is established by Shri Bhagavadpad and his great disciples, and Shri Sureshwara in his *Naishkarmya Siddhi* has built up a strong system of arguments in its support.

As the waves are only water and copper pots only copper, so the multitude of universes are the Self and the Self alone. [63]

In the philosophy of Advaita the unreality of the world and the reality of the Self are demonstrated in various ways and with the help of various illustrations. What are waves? Only water, and nothing but water. What are pots made of copper? Only copper and nothing else. So the world, in spite of its apparent diversity, is fundamentally nothing but the principle of consciousness.

Let it be carefully noted that the world is not a modification of the spirit. Advaita is not the philosophy of Spinoza, which postulates the reality of the world as an aspect of the spirit, the two combining together to make the divine substance. In the philosophy of Ramanuja Acharya the world is said to be real and not fundamentally different from the universal spirit; the animate and the inanimate together make up the spirit.

In Shri Shankara's philosophy, the world is a phenomenal superimposition (vivarta) on the Self. This fact is logically demonstrated by Gaudapada Acharya and other great Acharyas such as Swami Vidyaranya, and it is verified in experience by the sage who enters into the intuitive perception of the unity of Jiva, Brahman and jagat.

Man has not fallen : there is no such thing as original sin for which each and every man has to atone on earth. It is the submission of the spirit to nescience (avidya) which creates the relative consciousness, but the world loses its sting of fear when it is known to be phenomenal like a snake in a rope.

> *As by a jar is meant the clay and by cloth the threads of which it is composed, so by the name of the world is denoted consciousness ; negate the world and know it.* [64]

The world spread out in time and space, as well as the senses and mind through which it is cognised, is in truth nothing but consciousness, called Brahman in its universal aspect and Atman in its individual aspect. All our pain and misery, our greed and moral infirmities, are the result of the confusion of Brahman with the world. It is not hard to understand that the world has no independent existence. The world of material objects is full of contradictions when viewed by many individuals. Contradiction is the evidence of unreality. It is Brahman which, when cognised through the mind and the senses, appears as the world. Brahman is obscured, but not entirely. Who can deny the existence of the existent, the ability to appear or to be known which is inherent in objects ? The inner light which reveals the existence (Sat) in the objects is never obscured ; but when the mind confounds them with reality, duality, pain and suffering arise.

This verse contains a great metaphysical truth, and it is meant to be a text for daily meditation. The object of acquiring learning is to cognise the truth of the Self as the basis of the world. From duality our mind should be led to unity and from unity to transcendence. This is the method by which Brahman is intuitively cognised.

It may be asked: " Is not the world Maya ? Why is it called Brahman ? " Maya means erroneous cognition. When names and forms are taken as real and Brahman is not cognised, then that which is really and fundamentally Brahman is called Maya or jagat. The negation of the empirical consciousness and its absorption in the consciousness absolute leads to the knowledge of Brahman as the only reality and truth.

Whatever is done by man is based on the existence of Brahman, but overcome by ignorance man does not realize this. In fact all vessels made of clay are nothing but clay. [65]

Brahman is existence absolute : as nothing can be conceived to exist without existence, so nothing can take place without Brahman. When the rope is taken for the illusory snake, it is certain that all the bodily members of the snake, its dimensions, its colour and other seeming properties, are nothing but the rope. Brahman is all. It is ignorance which gives man an idea of separateness. One illusion leads to another and so on. Egoity is born as a result of the ignorance of Brahman, and from egoity arises the whole psychic equipment of man, and the world as well.

When the truth is known, duality disappears. Just as all fear caused by the appearance of the illusory snake ends when the rope is known, so all the pains and woes of the world end when Brahman is known.

Spinoza says that the highest good of man is the knowledge of the unity of all objects in one substance, and not intellectual knowledge. It is the knowledge of one's Self.

The Self is ever pure, yet it ever appears impure, just as the same rope appears in two aspects—as a rope for the one who knows and as a snake for the one who does not. [68]

For the spiritually enlightened sage Brahman is both the cause and effect of the universe, while to the man of limited vision on account of nescience (avidyā) Brahman appears as jagat, a conglomeration of change, destructibility and multiplicity in non-duality. The view of the ignorant creates fear and innumerable troubles and pain.

The same applies to the man who believes his Self to be the body, and this view too is the cause of innumerable sufferings. Those who want to pass from error to truth must realise the Self and enjoy peace and bliss as their own Self forever.

> *To a person on board a moving ship everything on the bank seems to be in motion ; similarly through nescience a man sees the body-form as his Self.* [76]

In order to strengthen the conviction that the Self is different from the body, another illustration is given. In succeeding verses, which are here omitted, the holy Acharya cites yet other illustrations to bring home the conviction of the truth to qualified disciples.

> *In the Shastra it is said that after Self-realization the prarabdha karma (that portion of our accumulated karma whose fruition has begun) still does not leave the jnani. We now refute this view.* [90]

It is a widespread belief that a knower of Self must experience the effects of his prarabdha karma. The potter may cease to give motion to his wheel and remove the staff with which he does so ; yet the wheel will still continue to revolve for a time under the momentum of the potter's last blow.

The doctrine of prarabdha is assumed by many of the great Acharyas, but it is only an explanatory doctrine and not an ultimate fact in the holy philosophy. For the student of average intelligence it throws light on many problems and furnishes an explanation as to why and how the self-realised man lives on in sansara, but it is not the ultimate truth. As in common parlance we say that the sun rises and sets, though in fact this is not so, so the doctrine of prarabdha is held to explain the outer life of the jnani, though the truth is that Atman neither performs karma of any kind, nor is bound by any of its results.

When the sleeper awakes, the dream disappears completely ; similarly the prarabdha, being unreal, ceases to exist on the rise of Self-knowledge. [91]

Prarabdha is not real : all experience in the form of waking, dreaming and dreamless sleep is a phenomenon caused by Maya. The very fact that it disappears and that each of the three states contradicts the other two proves its unreality. Shri Swami Satchitananda first brought to my notice the significance of this doctrine and refuted prarabdha with vigorous reasoning.

The karma performed in previous lives is called prarabdha ; but since in the conviction of the jnani there have been no previous lives, the prarabdha karma has no meaning. [92]

In a dream a man sees himself performing actions, meritorious and unmeritorious, and expects to reap the harvest he has sown ; but when he wakes up, the dream and its contents are no more. The same applies to the actions of the jnani. Jnana is the termination of the state of sansara, which in some important aspects is comparable to a dream. The realization of the nature of the Self as Sat-chit-ananda means the termination of the whole dream of sansara with its actions meritorious and otherwise. In the waking state that follows the dream no part of the dream remains. So how could the prarabdha karma continue to function after jnana ? The doctrine of prarabdha is a tentative one and is meant to explain certain methods to the beginner in the holy Yoga ; but in fact when all the karmas end, the prarabdha karma ends with them.

As a man under a delusion sees a snake in place of a rope, so the dull-witted, ignorant of the spiritual truth, see sansara instead of the truth. [95]

As on the perception of the rope the illusory snake disappears entirely, so when the substratum of the world (Brahman) is known, the whole world disappears as if non-existent. [96]

The body too is a detail in sansara, and when the whole of sansara ends on the rise of true cognition of the nature of Self, prarabdha disappears also. The holy Shruti gives the theory of prarabdha for the instruction of the unenlightened. (97)

Now I declare for the attainment of the cognition of truth fifteen stages (anga) of meditation (nididhyasana), which should be practised all the time by the candidate for spiritual illumination. [100]

Without constant practice one cannot achieve a cognition of the Self, which is reality and pure consciousness. To acquire the highest good the enquirer must therefore practise meditation on Brahman for a very long time. [101]

After listening and cogitation (shravana and manana) on the great spiritual dicta of the Veda, one who has disciplined his mind and given full devotion to his Guru must meditate on Brahman for a long time to acquire the spiritual illumination. The value of meditation is emphasised by the holy Acharya because by this mental process the nescience which has its locum in the Self is slowly destroyed.

The highest good is the complete cessation of all sufferings and the achievement of unity with the universal consciousness. Any other achievement is in the region of nescience (avidya) and does not annihilate the darkness through which the real appears as unreal and vice versa.

The meditation must be done for a long time, morning and evening, at fixed times, and an undercurrent in the mental consciousness of the Yogi in the form of " I am Brahman, not the body and the mind " must continue throughout the day. To devote time to pleasure, gossip or social intercourse of a purely superficial nature, is not only a waste of time but a very harmful practice. Friends who are pure empiricists are unreliable and do not help the higher way of life. To leave the spiritual way in order to please them is great folly—nay, it is dangerous too.

Shri Vidyaranya Swami says: "Let a man meditate on Brahman or talk about Brahman to one or more. This is called the practice of Brahman." The knowledge of Brahman is not to be inflicted on anybody, nor to be made an object of show. Life in a spiritual group (Sangha) is important for many reasons, one of which is the opportunities it gives for conversing on the truth with fellow Yogis.

It is folly to try to convert anybody to the Yogic way of life unless he wants to live as a good man and acquire the holy knowledge. People often marry a partner thinking they will change him or her. But alas, this rarely happens.

The following in proper order and sequence are the stages of Yoga: outer control (yama), inner control (niyama), renunciation (tyaga), observance of silence (mauna), place (desha), time (kala), posture (asana), control of the nervous system (mulabandha), stability of the body (dehasamya), position of the eyes (drik-sthiti), breath-control (pranayama), withdrawal of the sense-organs from their objects (pratyahara), constant meditation (dharana), causal meditation (dhyana) and samadhi. [102 and 103]

The holy Acharya, basing his instruction on the deepest spiritual teachings of the Upanishads and the unwritten ones which he received from his own Guru Deva, here explains and interprets the stages

of Yoga. They are different from those given by
the holy sage Patanjali and deserve very careful
study and practice. Here is the Yoga which is the
real Adhyatma Yoga, and its followers must give it
their single-minded allegiance and avoid the troubles
inherent in other conceptions of Yoga. This is the
Yoga which Paramahansa Swami Krishnanandaji,
Shri Dada Bhagavan, Shri Rama Tirtha and others,
have followed. It is quite adequate to give the
full realization of Self to a devoted disciple.

> *Outer control (yama) is the regulation of the sense
> functions by the knowledge " Verily, all is
> Brahman." This practice should be long continued.*
> [104]

The practice of meditation with deep feeling on
" Verily, all is Brahman " means the negation of
names and forms as unreal and concentration on
the existence, on which names and forms are
imposed, as Brahman. This great step in the holy
Adhyatma Yoga is called yama.

This meditation consists in a thorough understanding of the holy dictum " Verily, all is Brahman " and then in applying its practical aspect to
our daily life. There is no friend and no foe, no
heaven and no hell, nothing to be desired and
nothing to be given up, because all is one—that is,
Brahman. This is the conviction that has to be
matured. It is to be based on faith in the same way
as a geometrical proposition or chemical formula is
first accepted on trust and afterwards subjected to
verification. This is the highest psychological

practice and is above all psycho-analytic or any other psychiatric methods.

About fifty years ago the great German thinkers Ernest Haeckel and Planck reduced the variety of nature to unity. The holy Yoga ordains that the unity is spiritual. Matter is merely a term which is indefinable, and nobody really knows what it means.

All complexes, frustrations, mental restrictions and inhibitions are destroyed by the concept " All is Brahman ". It should be dwelt on mentally for a long time every day and for as long as we can in our practical life. A true disciple must be ready to make any sacrifice, social, economic, domestic or otherwise, to carry on this continuous stream of thought in the depth of his mind. This is the surest way to the control of the senses. When the mental trend is changed, the operation of the senses changes automatically. No arguments to fatigue our brain, no study of the classics which are not based on pure Advaita, no adherence to the pseudo-teachers, who are bitten by the snake of the desire for fame and for being thought original, is to be entertained even for a moment.

Some might say : " Shall we not learn from everybody ? " No. We have to learn from those who are competent to teach ; otherwise we will be consumed in the fire of ambition of the pseudo-teachers.

To encourage the flow of the unitive vrittis and to restrain the separative is inner control (niyama), of the nature of supreme bliss ; the wise practise it with fixed determination. [105]

A very important principle is involved in this declaration. It means that the mind is teachable and tractable. Here it is stressed that to acquire the supreme good, the sattvic vrittis of the mind, such as patience, devotion, faith, forgiveness, love of study and so forth, are the modes of the mind which must be cultivated and that the modifications which are obstructions to the supreme realization of truth as Self, such as pleasure and power desires, materialism, lassitude, egoism and the habit of destructive criticism, pursuit of national fanaticism, self-importance, hatred or dislike of others under any circumstances, procrastination of good intentions, are the vrittis which must be curbed. How? Mental violence will not do. To curb a harmful vritti, the Yogi entertains its opposite with patience. This is the only way to the inner and real peace, the peace which needs no outer object for its creation or its maintenance. The wise, those who have a spiritual end of life in view, cultivate the subjective discipline with determination and according to the rules.

> To regard the created world as consciousness and to renounce its appearance as unreal is the true renunciation (tyaga); it is honoured by the great because it gives release at once. [106]

This is the real meaning of renunciation in the holy Adhyatma Yoga. It does not mean flight from society by seeking refuge in woods and caves far away from the world of men. Renunciation is a subjective quality, and its real spirit, as defined in this verse, is to think the world nothing but consciousness absolute and to regard all names and forms as unreal. It is opposed to the conception of the pseudo-Vedantic thinkers who believe that the world is a snare which can be avoided by having recourse to a life of inactivity and poverty. Even those who have run away from the world have been known to be attached to renunciation, fame and power; besides, we have to face the facts and not be sentimental about renunciation.

This is a most important verse; it gives the real teaching of the holy Acharya on renunciation, which is to regard the world as consciousness itself.

Take the case of a deluded man who, watching the waves break upon the sea-shore, takes them to be real. He is happy when he sees them rise higher and higher but sighs when he sees them break. He calls the bubbles beautiful and the breakers destructive. Such a man is neither free nor happy; but when he learns that the waves, breakers and bubbles are nothing but water, he becomes free from joy over their rise and grief over their fall. Then he is called a renunciate.

Swami Nirbhyanandaji has said that he who prides himself on his renunciation is as ignorant as one who is attached to the world.

That from which mind and speech turn back baffled is the silence (mauna) accessible only to the Yogis; that the wise become. [107]

Silence (mauna) is one of the great spiritual practices which lead to the realization of the Self. It is misunderstood by the pseudo-Yogis, who interpret it as observance of physical silence and refrain from speaking. Such silence by itself has no value. A Yogi named Ramanandaji, whom I met in Sambhal in 1903 when he was an old man, had kept physical silence for twelve years but had eventually given it up as it had done him no spiritual good; he confessed that it had given him a false pride from the stern discipline it involved. Some people observe silence but indicate their desires by writing. This is sheer hypocrisy. Unless the mind is silenced and restrained from material desires by the knowledge of Vedanta, mere physical dumbness is only an imitation of the cow and does no spiritual good. The real silence is the contemplation of the higher Self as " I am That ", because the mind and the senses cannot approach it and in fact derive their individuation from it. In this spiritual discipline of the contemplation of the Self as the inspirer of the mind and speech and as the universal essence of beauty and virtue lies the real meaning of silence.

Who can describe That (Brahman) from which all words turn away? Even the world is beyond the range of words. [108]

A subtle aspect of the holy truth is given in this verse. The object which is either real or unreal is subject to speech, whereas that which is neither real nor unreal cannot be described. The world as time, space and causation disappears in the state of the knowledge of truth, and therefore it is not real ; but because it is subject to cognition in the state of nescience it cannot be called unreal. The world therefore, being neither real nor unreal, is termed indescribable (anirvachaniya). Besides, the relation between the sound and the objects which it denotes is purely imaginary. Emmanuel Kant has discussed the subject and proved the existence of the phenomenon to be mere imagination.

This then is the real silence of the wise, known as the natural silence (sahaja); the silence of the lips is prescribed by the knowers of Brahman only for the dull-witted. [109]

Man's attitude to any object in this world ultimately resolves into " I do not know it ". The physical sciences investigate the appearance of objects and honestly describe them as mysterious, and knowable only up to a point.

For physical life it is useful to know the laws of nature and so be able to control its forces. The value of such a knowledge is mostly utilitarian. From the spiritual point of view, all that we can say about nature is : " We do not know ".

Words can express little, and very few have the power to use words rightly and adequately. It is only the ignorant who boast of knowledge. Real learning is accompanied by the extension of ignorance and is nothing more than the pursuit of reality in the phenomenon. Shortly before his death, that most philosophical and prolific of writers, St. Thomas Aquinas, laid down his pen and became silent. What other way is there to

express reality in the spiritual state of satisfaction ?
In fact, the less we speak, the better we know.

Swami Mangalnathji spoke just as many words
as were necessary to express his thought and no
more. The highest fruit of speech is adoration of
the Lord and communication of dharma ; both
require few words. Holy Christ was as economical
in words as the Lord Buddha.

> *That place (desha) is called solitary by which the
> universe is ever pervaded and in which there is no one
> either in the beginning, the middle or the end.* [110]

In the beginning of Yogic life solitude is recommended ; the society of people with many worldly
interests is a hindrance to spiritual contemplation.
But this is only a preliminary state. The real
solitary place is Brahman ; in Him nothing really
exists, and He pervades every atom of the universe.
To dwell mentally on Brahman as the only all-
pervasive reality symbolised as OM is to abide in
loneliness. Engrossed in the pursuit of virtue or
the adoration of beauty a man can feel lonely even
in the midst of society. The holy *Gita* was preached
by the Lord of the universe in the thick of battle.
It is a mental weakness to be afraid of society when
dharma requires one to be in it.

> *Because of its creation (kalana) in a second of all
> beings beginning with Brahma, the secondless part-
> less bliss is denoted by the word kala (time).* [111]

In some schools of Yoga great importance is
attached to time (kala). According to one school

kala is even identified with God. It is in opposition
to this view that the most holy Acharya shows that
if kala has any existence at all it is dependent upon
Brahman. In the holy Adhyatma Yoga kala is just a
modification of Prakriti and not a creative agent.

> *The inner state which permits the uninterrupted*
> *contemplation of Brahman is to be considered the*
> *best posture (asana) ; this is the real posture, and*
> *not others which merely disturb one's ease.* [112]

In Hatha Yoga and the Yoga of Patanjali much
stress is laid on the posture in which the Yogi
should sit for meditation. Yogi Gorakshanath has
given eighty-four postures. They are not all
intended for meditation ; some are merely physical
exercises to improve the health and give nervous
relaxation. The holy Yoga is called Adhyatma
(spiritual) because its practices are independent of
physical exercises.

The holy Acharya here defines posture ; it is an
inner state in which the Yogi can contemplate the
all-pervasiveness of Brahman. Bergson says that
duration is apprehended by intuition. The all-
pervasiveness of Self can be reflected upon in the
state of higher meditation in which, after some
practice, the contemplation becomes continuous.
This is called posture (asana) in Adhyatma Yoga.

> *That which is the first cause of all beings, the*
> *imperishable substratum of the universe, in which*
> *the perfect Yogis abide, is called the perfect*
> *posture (siddhasana).* [113]

Among the postures recommended for meditation, siddhasana is the chief one. It is variously described in the non-Adhyatmic Yogas. Some pseudo-Yogis have woven a net of radiations, vibrations and nervous currents to explain the advantages of a sitting posture ; but in the holy Adhyatma Yoga all physical means are considered unimportant. This point is to be thoroughly understood by the students of Advaita Vedanta. Shri Dada once remarked when asked about the state of samadhi which a Yogi is taught to attain : " My holy Guru was in samadhi when he seemed to be teaching, studying, walking and reading". One of the greatest services done by Shankaracharya to the practice of spirituality was to free it from the emphasis on physical methods. It is only charlatans who insist on the use of physical means to accomplish spiritual ends.

That which is the root of all beings and supported on which the mind can be made restful, that mula-bandha is ever to be practised ; this is the Yoga of the Raja Yogis. [114]

In Hatha Yoga and in some Raja Yogas mulabandha (the control of the root) is held to be a very important process in the achievement of samadhi. In some Yogas it has to do with the root of the spinal column and the control of the arteries and veins which surround it ; but in the Adhyatma Yoga the holy Acharya has dispensed with all such physical practices and has ignored all the chakras and so forth. This Yoga is purely spiritual, and the method is mental and meditative.

When the mind is fully absorbed in the contempla-
tion of Brahman, the state following this absorption
is called equilibrium (samata). The mere
straightening of the limbs like those of a withered
tree is not equilibrium. [115]

In certain Yogas stress is laid on effecting the
equilibrium of the members of the body by starva-
tion and other similar physical practices. This is
neither essential nor very useful. The real samata
is the absorption of the activities of the mind in the
contemplation of Brahman.

The mind is affected by certain physical con-
tortions, but in the holy Adhyatma Yoga these
practices are not accepted and the mind is brought
under control by mental discipline and not by
physical means.

Make thy vision the vision of illumination
(jnanamayi) and see the world (jagat) as Brahman:
this is the supreme vision and not to look at the
tip of the nose. [116]

In other systems of Yoga you are asked to concentrate on the tip of your nose, on the navel or on
a part of your head. In the beginning of the
practice of Yoga, when you are learning how to
concentrate, such exercises have some value. They
stimulate certain venous centres and create a feeling
of peace, but this feeling is temporary and is not
the bliss of Self-knowledge. In the holy Adhyatma
Yoga the whole process of perception is revolu-
tionised by discrimination born of the study of
Vedanta. The Yogi tries to negate that which is

ephemeral in objects, their name and form aspect ; and when that is negated, what remains is Brahman. Steady practice, accompanied by non-attachment and renunciation, leads the intellect to the contemplation of the world as Self. When this contemplation is matured, you have the realization of Self, accompanied by eternal peace and bliss, complete fearlessness and love of all creatures as your own Self. Concentrating on the tip of the nose is only for backward students.

> *The restraint of all the modifications of the mind through meditating on them as Brahman in all the forms of chitta and so forth is called breath control (pranayama).* [118]

It is a common error that pranayama or breath control, which is scientifically explained by the holy Sage Patanjali and has been vulgarised in many American methods, is essential for Self-realization. It is useful if done properly under a competent teacher, but it is not essential. The holy Yoga is purely spiritual, and the approach recommended in it is through a controlled mind set on devotion and meditation.

Shri Dada hardly ever spoke of pranayama. Let us dismiss it and find the best means to Self-realization not in breath control but in shravana, manana and nididhyasana.

> *To negate the reality of matter and its transformations is the outgoing breath (rechaka) of pranayama. The vritti " I am Brahman " is called the ingoing breath (puraka) of pranayama.* [119]

Here is an explanation of the three modes of pranayama (breath control). The first is to exhale slowly and to keep the lungs empty ; this is called rechaka. The second is to take slowly a deep breath till the lungs are filled ; this is called puraka. In the holy Adhyatma Yoga these are not primarily physical exercises ; they are exercises in the manipulation of the mind designed to create the vrittis : " The world is unreal, it has no real existence " (rechaka) and " Verily, I am Brahman " (puraka).

> To make the mental mode " I am Brahman " stable is called kumbhaka. This is the real method of pranayama for the wise ; painful breathing exercises are for the ignorant. [120]

The third mode of pranayama is the kumbhaka, which means slowly taking a deep breath and holding it as long as convenient. The holy Acharya makes it clear that pranayama is a spiritual exercise and not a physical one. Those who look for any worldly advantage and imagine that they can secure it by breath control may do the pranayama as taught by Rishi Patanjali, but those who want spiritual illumination need not go into these painful physical processes.

> To consider the sense-objects as the Self and to merge the mind in consciousness is called the practice of the withdrawal of the sense-organs from their respective objects (pratyahara). The Mumukshus are instructed to practise this process and not its physical counterpart. [121]

This verse gives the spiritual exercise to supersede the physical practice of Yoga called pratyahara. Every object of the senses is to be considered as the Self, and the mind is finally to be absorbed in the contemplation of the infinite consciousness as the Self. When this higher mental state is matured, then nothing further remains to be practised or achieved.

> Constant meditation (dharana) is to know Brahman as the substratum of the object of thought and to still the mind in that knowledge. [122]

In Yoga, dharana, which means a matured form of meditative vision, is considered an important part of the inner life. A tapestry of imagination is woven round dharana in the Yoga of Patanjali and in other Yogas. In the holy Adhyatma Yoga, as expounded by Shri Bhagavadpad Shankara, all imaginative practices connected with dharana are dismissed as elementary and preparatory. The main purpose of dharana is to see Brahman as the substratum of any object of thought in the realm of time-space. It is a matter of practice. The Yogi sits practising introspection, that is to say, watching the functions of his mind. He is not attached to appearances but to the reality, the pure consciousness on which appearances are phenomenally superimposed like the shapes of golden ornaments on gold. If this practice is joined with devoted love of Guru and Govinda, the mind is purified, and the vision of transcendent unity in the form of " I am Brahman " dawns and stays for ever.

The state of complete independence that is produced by the true vritti " I am Brahman " is called causal meditation (dhyana) and gives the highest joy. [123]

How puzzling is the word ' meditation ' (dhyana) to a novice in Yoga ! Some pseudo-Yogis have used it in an imaginative sense of their own ; others have linked it to the practice of ' piercing the chakras ' as it is called. Let us brush aside all methods of this type. The beautiful dreams of the poets, unless based on pure bhakti, are also useless as forms of meditation.

The real truth of meditation is revealed in this verse by the compassionate Acharya. Let us still the mind by the practice of selfless benevolence to the creatures of God, by upasana and renunciation. Then it is easy to create the vritti " Verily, I am Brahman ". When this vritti arises, the supreme purpose of life is achieved. The doors of spiritual illumination are open. All dreams of sin and sorrow, virtue and weakness, end. This is real meditation.

The samadhi of spiritual illumination (jnana) is the state of consciousness in which the vritti, which has assumed the form of Brahman and become change-less, loses its vritti-hood. [124]

This verse defines the high water-mark of the mental condition, after which the vritti which consists of two entities, Brahman and avidya, loses its avidyahood and the Jiva is transformed within and without, in and above time and space, into one homogeneous consciousness. This is the very perfection of the mental consciousness.

This verse explains the highest state of Yogic samadhi. There are people like Plotinus, the neo-Platonist, who say that they obtain samadhi (what his biographer Porphyry calls the state of trance) and then lose it. In the last volume of his Philosophy of History, Dr. Arnold Toynbee speaks of a similar spiritual experience, in which he says the true meaning of history was revealed to him. The real samadhi of Adhyatma Yoga is the negation of nescience and the revelation of the Self as Sat-chit-ananda which, when once experienced, abides for ever. It stands to reason that the man who has once seen the rope is never again subject to illusion.

Only one who himself has spiritual experience will understand the real meaning of this verse. Students of Yoga are asked to meditate upon it deeply.

A man should practise the achievement of the natural bliss of samadhi till, by throwing his mind into it even for a second, he experiences the incomparable bliss. [125]

The real meaning of this verse is not easy to comprehend, but the grace of Shri Dada accomplishes what the intellect never can. It means that the Yogi keeps the state of supreme realization. By withdrawing his vritti from the objects, not materially but psychically, he can remain in the highest state. He becomes master of the state of samadhi.

Let it be clearly noted that in the state of the

F   73

highest samadhi no activity such as teaching or writing is possible. Yet the Yogi who has seen the Self within and the Self without keeps his individuality under perfect control and makes use of it for spiritual purposes. The vritti is at his command; it has lost its power of limitation. This is a great secret of Adhyatma Yoga, to understand which fully you must have the advantage of the grace of your Guru. Not in many places is this great secret revealed, even by the great Acharyas.

When the king of Yogis, rising above all the means and practices of Self-illumination, becomes his own Self, his state is such that it cannot be conceived by the mind nor described in speech. [126]

This verse is most illuminating. Some great avadhuts like Rama Tirtha may give involuntary expression to their state of Self-illumination; but it is never voluntary. Swami Nirbhyanandaji said, when pressed to describe the state of the attainment of the spiritual samadhi: " I know it, but I can't explain it. My Guru, by making a gesture, revealed the Self unto my Self ". This is the highest expression that can be used. Note that a ' gesture ' is used by the Guru; it is neither by arguments nor by syllogisms that the nature of the Self is revealed by the Guru. The word ' gesture ' implies something indefinable. Some say that the Self is revealed by a symbol. It is not so. When the disciple who has thrown aside the burden of egoity and crushed desire and aversion under his feet, feels spiritually at one with the Guru, then God in the Guru reveals Himself to God in the disciple. This realization is beyond all description.

> *The obstacles in the way of the practice of samadhi arise with force and certainty. Among them the principal are lethargy, pointless thoughts undevoted to the holy ideal, desire for enjoyment of the sense-objects, absorption (laya), darkness (tamas), agitation (vikshepa), desire for flavour (rasasvada), mental vacuity (shunyata) and so forth. A practicant of the divine Yoga should overcome them slowly and with determination.* [127 and 128]

Progress towards the spiritual ideal is not continuous ; there are rises and falls on the way. Every step is beset with difficulties and dangers which can only be surmounted by great vigilance and determination.

Some of the chief obstacles in the way of the practice of samadhi are mentioned in this verse. One is the desire for rest and the inclination to postpone, under various pretences, the spiritual exercises and the leading of a life of dharma and sacrifice. This must be overcome. Another subtle impediment on the path of Yoga is the desire to enjoy the delights of sense-objects, and this may take the form of invasions of sex-feelings or desires for holidays in the mountains or sight-seeing tours. Sometimes the mind falls into a state of inactivity, and the Yogi begins to think that he has reached the goal and that the fruit of realization will follow.

At other times a very strong obstacle is mental vacuity when the negative work of the elimination of the passions and of restlessness seems to have been done, and a feeling of negation supervenes in the mind; although this state is accompanied by a certain peace and detachment, still the positive side of Yoga, the bliss of illumination, is missing. To keep a spiritual diary and to go through it and to form the habit of deep introspection are helpful practices recommended by the Saint Universal.

Those who take the Yoga half-heartedly find their entire life one great obstacle. They think their worldly duties far more important than their spiritual duty. Wholehearted devotion to Guru and Govinda is helpful in such cases.

In the course of the practice of samadhi (objectless meditation on the Self) positive feelings may arise, or in the case of the absence of vritti the state of vacuity; but in the case of meditation on perfection (purnata), perfection is realised. [129]

This verse will be understood by those who have made appreciable progress in the practice of samadhi. It should be carefully studied and pondered upon.

In the state of deep meditation on the Absolute the mind sometimes assumes the form of positive feelings; in that case such vrittis as " I am all ", " I have all ", may present themselves to the Yogi. At other times there is the vritti of emptiness, perfect vacuity; there is nothing positive and nothing negative in this vritti; the Yogi wrongly imagines that this is the ideal. He should meditate on completeness, self-sufficiency, perfect wantlessness and spiritual perfection. Unless there is deep vairagya, this state cannot be imagined. Only those who have devoted their whole egoity to Guru and Govinda will understand the deep significance of this verse.

It is most compassionate of the holy Acharya to unfold these mystical teachings in this short classic.

Those who do not strive for this highly pure Brahman-vritti live in vain ; though men in appearance, they are in fact as beasts. [130]

They are good people who know the value of this vritti and promote it. They are blessed and worthy of adoration in the three worlds. [131]

Those who have developed this Brahman-vritti to its full maturity acquire the superior state of Brahmanhood. This high spiritual state is not accessible to those who merely talk of it and do not work for it. [132]

Through discipline, devotion and the diminution of egoity, the vritti which first appears as great shanti and universal love can be matured into perfect Brahmanhood as " I am Shiva ", " I am Shiva ".

There are people who begin to feel the inner peace and joy of the life of meditation and devotion carried on single-mindedly irrespective of obstructions, but unless they are very careful and persevering and guard themselves from the appeal of sense-pleasures, particularly sex-delight, fame and power, their vritti is likely to be dragged down. This is a critical moment in the life of a Yogi. Complete devotion to Guru and the practice of vairagya are a great help.

> *Those who are clever and skilful in talking of Vedanta but are devoid of the Brahman-vritti and are devoted to the objects of the sense-pleasures ought to be considered extremely ignorant. They are born and they die again and again.* [133]

It is neither blind faith nor the mere use of the tongue in loose and indiscriminate discussion of the theories of Vedanta that leads to release. Those who follow this course, though they may write voluminous books on Indian philosophy, remain highly ignorant. The interest in Brahmavidya must be accompanied by complete detachment, renunciation, devotion and the practice of general benevolence. Those who lack these qualities may enjoy fame as scholars and occupy chairs of philosophy in noted universities, but they have no real merit as jnanis, and they will be born again and again in sansara to reap the harvest of their karma.

A simple man, pure in heart, practising renunciation and compassion and devoted to the practice and study of the holy Adhyatma Yoga, is far superior to a learned scholar who is a sceptic at heart and writes and talks of Vedanta only to win fame.

78

The real Yogis are like Brahma, Sanaka and Paramahansa Shuka, who do not forsake the vritti of Brahman even for a moment. [134]

The effect is imagined in the cause, but the cause does not necessarily contain the effect. Through reflection (vichara) the effect is negated, and then the cause is no longer called a cause. [135]

A profound spiritual truth is contained in this verse. The world, the phenomenal existence, inheres in its cause, the substratum (Brahman), but when by the power of constant meditation and reflection the effect is negated as unreal, the cause also ceases to be a cause. The meaning is that when the unreality of the phenomenal existence is fully realised, Brahman is no longer considered as the cause of the world. It is the effect which makes Brahman appear as the cause, but through study and logical reflection the existence of the world independent of Brahman is seen to be merely apparent. In this way, by meditation and deep reflection in a stilled and purified heart, the Yogi realises the absoluteness of Brahman. Nothing remains to be achieved or to be done.

That which is inaccessible to speech is called pure. This should be meditated upon in connection with the illustration of the clay and the jar. [136]

The word ' pure ' (shuddha) in Vedanta philosophy is not used in a moral, chemical or theological sense. It refers to something in which there is no participation of any other entity whatsoever. The jar, as an entity separate from the clay, is merely a name; so is the world in relation to the Self (Atman). This is the way we should meditate and reflect on Yogic lines. When the mind understands this truth, it becomes no mind, just as the jar, when understood in its essence, loses its jarhood and is seen to be only clay. A deep truth is contained in these verses.

> *When a man follows this method, the vṛitti assumes the form of Brahman; then in that pure heart arises the light of the knowledge of truth.* [137]

The process of the holy Adhyatma Yoga is one of inner tranquillity, peace of devotion, rise of the vritti of unity of the Self with God and finally realization of the identity of the Self with Brahman. It is by real devotion to the Yoga and detachment from worldly achievements that the vritti in the state of deep meditation is turned into the form of Brahman.

Cognition is the result of the transformation of the vritti into the object cognised. Thus by fixed and devoted meditation on "All is Brahman" the vritti becomes Brahman. In this state there is a certain awareness of external objects, but they appear as if in a dream. Then follows the realization of the identity of Jiva and Brahman, which is the highest state of divine illumination.

> *The Yogis first separate the cause from the effect and then see the cause in the effect.* [138]

This is another method of Yogic meditation and it is a very high one. It involves two psychological processes : first, the world is seen as the effect and the Self as the cause ; and second, Brahman in the state of meditation is seen as pervading the world and in fact as one with the world, just as the clay is one with the jar. These are most valuable methods of meditation and are given in the simplest possible form by the holy and compassionate Acharya.

> *Let the Yogi first see the cause in the effect and then give up the conception of the effect. In this way the significance of cause also disappears and the Yogi, freed from the causal relationship, acquires the form of that which remains.* [139]

This is another most useful form of meditation and a conception to be kept in mind all the time by a devout Yogi. He first sees the cause in the effect—that is, Brahman in the world—and then he forgets the effect—that is, in his deep meditation he negates the world as a shadow or a dream. In this way he rises above the domain of cause and effect. When the causal relationship is negated, what remains ? Brahman, Reality, the Self of the individual and the universe. This is the highest state.

> *Whatever a man thinks of steadfastly and with unshakable conviction, that he soon becomes. The story of the bee and the worm illustrates this clearly.* [140]

The Shruti says : " A man is what he thinks himself to be ". That human thought is creative and leads to goodness if directed to good channels but that it quickly degenerates if its cultivation is neglected or if it is directed to evil objects and ideas, was known to the holy sages of the Himalayas long before Aristotle wrote his thoughts on psychology. This fact has been emphasised in the Gita Shastra and elsewhere in the holy literature. The holy sage Ashtavakra says : " What a man thinks of that he becomes ". This is important to remember.

For our own good we must guide our mind and lead it to the contemplation of truth and beauty. This is the secret of prayer. The man who devotes his precious mental energy to hate, love of ease and comfort, sex delights and pursuit of power, is wasting the supreme capital of his mind-energy on nothing.

The illustration of the bee and the worm is as follows. A bee catches a worm and shuts it up alive in a tiny hole. In the course of time the bee returns. When the hole is opened, a bee straightway flies out. The worm by constant and uninterrupted meditation on the bee has become a bee itself.*

This whole world in its visible and invisible form is consciousness. The wise man should every day meditate carefully on his Self. [141]

The world has two aspects, visible and invisible, material and spiritual, perishable and eternal. The

* This is a traditional legend.

Self which is imperishable, being the substratum of the organs of conception and perception, must ever be heard about, thought of and meditated upon.

The instinctive realm is the lowest of the planes of existence. It has a utilitarian value, but it must be kept subordinate to the spiritual value. We make a fire in order to cook our meal on it ; we sleep, eat and carry on other physical activities ultimately to promote our spiritual good.

> *The wise man should mentally transform the seen into the unseen and meditate upon it as Brahman. Engaging his intellect in the tranquil and perfect delight of consciousness, he should abide in eternal felicity.* [142]

This is the Yogic practice and the abiding intellectual attitude of the Yogi towards the world. As a diamond lies hidden in a coal-mine, so God is present as consciousness and bliss in every intellect. His bliss aspect can be brought out through the firm conviction of the reality of God and the unreality of the world and by converging the many lines of mental life on the one great truth " Verily, all is Brahman ". No attempts to understand this truth intellectually will be fruitful, but, in a way that the mind cannot grasp, the truth will shine forth in and through the intellect and the Yogi will be spiritually awakened. Then follows the state called jivanmukti. This is the highest goal, the normal state of consciousness ; this is truth.

*The Yoga composed of all the steps mentioned
here is called Raja Yoga. It will give spiritual
perfection to him who practises it, but if his mind
is not entirely free from desires he may combine
with it some aspects of Hatha Yoga. Nevertheless
he whose desires for worldly objects have ended will
attain full spiritual perfection through the practice
of this Yoga alone, untainted with Hatha Yoga.
This Yoga is easily accessible to all those who are
devoted to their Guru and to God.* [143 *and* 144]

By Hatha Yoga is meant not the revolting practices
of filling the intestines with gallons of water,
twisting and turning the tongue and so forth, but
the gentle methods of breath control (pranayama),
meditation postures and other practices formulated
by Shri Patanjali. The latter are not essential.
It is to strengthen the power of the will to live as
a Yogi and to persevere in the cause of virtue,
devotion and meditation under trying circumstances, both external and internal, that the special
methods of Shri Patanjali's Yoga are recommended.
Our desires for pleasure and power are great barriers
to spiritual peace. By the study of Vedanta and
by reflection on the objects of the world as unreal
and incapable of giving either peace or real lasting
delight, desires can be overcome. Besides, when
the delight in the form of shanti arising from the
practice of meditation and holy study is experienced,
worldly desires lose their charm and become stale.
If we live under the light of discrimination, we can
easily recognise the false delight which the worldly
objects cause. What thirsty man will run after a

river he knows to be a mirage ? The craving of the soul is satisfied only by devotion to God and Guru, by the practice of discipline and by self-dedication to the service of Vedanta. It should be noted carefully that devotion to Guru and to God is the key to success in the holy Yoga.

Thus ends the 'Direct Experience of Reality'.

GLOSSARY

ACHARYA   Teacher belonging to a traditional school of Yoga.

ADHYATMA   Concerning the Highest Self.

ADVAITA   Literally " Non-Duality ".   A school of Vedanta philosophy whose chief exponent was Shri Shankara, which teaches the oneness of the individual soul with God.

AJNANA   Absence of true knowledge, a synonym of avidya.

ANTAHKARANA   The " inner organ " of the individual, comprising the mind, emotions, intellect and the sense of ego ; that which makes up the individual personality.

ASAT   see " SAT".

ATMAN   The higher Self of man which is identical with the Supreme Reality (Brahman).

AVADHUT   A Sage who follows the path of withdrawal from the world, and lives as a renunciate.

AVIDYA   Nescience, or ignorance of the spiritual truth. The cause of suffering and bondage in the unenlightened.

BRAHMA   God, the Creator : the first person of the Hindu Trinity, the other two being Vishnu and Shiva.

BRAHMAN   God, the Absolute.   The Supreme Spirit.

CHAKRA   A centre of power in the physical body which can be awakened by certain practices.

CHITTA   Memory, imagination : one of the four functions of the mind.

DHARMA   Righteousness. Duty The basis of the rule of law in the world and of the individual's moral code.

GLOSSARY

GOVINDA   A name of Vishnu incarnated as Shri Krishna.

GURU   Spiritual Teacher. *Bringer of light*

JAGAT   The creation. Literally " the moving thing".

JIVA   The individual soul.

JIVANMUKTA   A liberated soul.

JIVANMUKTI   Spiritual liberation from the bonds of nescience: the state of one who has gained enlightenment during this life.

JNANA   Knowledge of Reality : enlightenment.

KARMA   Action and its consequences as determined by the law of cause and effect.
Prarabdha karma—that portion of karma whose fruition has already begun.

MAYA   The creative power (shakti) of the Lord which has brought the Universe into phenomenal existence.

MUMUKSHU   One who seeks liberation from the bonds of ignorance.

PRAKRITI   The primordial substance out of which both mind and matter have been evolved.

PRARABDHA   see " KARMA".

RAJAS   The principle of activity, passion or desire.

RISHI   A spiritually perfect Sage.

SAMADHI   A high state of consciousness in which the mind transcends the normal subject–object relationship.
Objectless meditation.

SAMATA   Equanimity. Serenity of mind.

SANSARA   The cycle of birth, death and rebirth involving experience of the phenomenal world.

GLOSSARY

Sᴀᴛ, Aѕᴀᴛ   Existence or Truth, Non-existence or unreality.

Sᴀᴛ–Cʜɪᴛ–Aɴᴀɴᴅᴀ   Existence–Consciousness–Bliss: three aspects of Brahman.   *Reality*

Sᴀᴛᴛᴡᴀ   The principle of light, harmony and happiness.

Sʜᴀɴᴛɪ   Spiritual peace, the inner peace experienced by a tranquillised mind.

Sʜᴀѕᴛʀᴀѕ   The recognised spiritual classics.

Sʜʀᴀᴠᴀɴᴀ, Mᴀɴᴀɴᴀ and Nɪᴅɪᴅʜʏᴀѕᴀɴᴀ   Listening to the spiritual Truth, reflection on it and uninterrupted contemplation of it with one-pointed concentration.

Sʜʀᴜᴛɪ   The divinely revealed scriptures.

Tᴀᴍᴀѕ   The principle of darkness, inertia and doubt.

Uᴘᴀѕᴀɴᴀ   Devotion to the Lord, worship.

Vᴀɪʀᴀɢʏᴀ   Desirelessness, non-attachment.

Vᴇᴅᴀɴᴛᴀ   The philosophy of the Vedas, which are the oldest Indian Scriptures.

Vɪᴄʜᴀʀᴀ   Enquiry into the spiritual Truth : cogitation.

Vɪᴅʏᴀ   Knowledge, a synonym of Jnana.

Vɪᴠᴀʀᴛᴀ   The phenomenal superimposition of an unreal appearance upon a real substratum, e.g., of the mirage water on the desert sand.   In particular, the phenomenal superimposition of the world on the Spirit.

Vʀɪᴛᴛɪ   A modification of the mind: an idea or thought complex.

Yᴏɢᴀ   Literally " Yoke " : the technique and discipline by which the individual soul (jiva) can achieve union with the Supreme Spirit (Brahman).

tine 66